Somerville Art Gallery

The collection of paintings by American and foreign artists,

formed by Mr. Sheperd Gandy, also other paintings

belonging to the estate of the late Mr. G. Talbot Olyphant

Somerville Art Gallery

The collection of paintings by American and foreign artists, formed by Mr. Sheperd Gandy, also other paintings belonging to the estate of the late Mr. G. Talbot Olyphant

ISBN/EAN: 9783337184711

Printed in Europe, USA, Canada, Australia, Japan

Cover: Foto ©Thomas Meinert / pixelio.de

More available books at **www.hansebooks.com**

PEREMPTORY SALE.

...

CATALOGUE

OF THE PRIVATE COLLECTION OF

MR. SHEPERD GANDY'S

PAINTINGS.

ALSO OTHERS BELONGING TO THE

ESTATE OF THE LATE MR. G. TALBOT OLYPHANT,

TO BE SOLD AT AUCTION.

Wednesday and Thursday Evenings,

MARCH 24TH AND 25TH,

AT THE

SOMERVILLE ART GALLERY,

82 Fifth Avenue.

THE COLLECTION

OF

PAINTINGS

BY

AMERICAN AND FOREIGN ARTISTS,

FORMED BY

MR. SHEPERD GANDY.

ALSO OTHER PAINTINGS BELONGING TO THE ESTATE OF THE LATE

MR. G. TALBOT OLYPHANT,

Sold to Close the Estates.

THE COLLECTION IS OF GREAT VARIETY AND EXCELLENCE, AND THE WORKS OF NEARLY

ONE HUNDRED ARTISTS ARE REPRESENTED,

THE WHOLE NOW ON EXHIBITION,

Day and Evening,

AT THE

Somerville Gallery,

82 FIFTH AVENUE,

WHERE THEY WILL BE SOLD WITHOUT RESERVE ON

Wednesday and Thursday Evenings, March 24th and 25th.

R. SOMERVILLE, Auctioneer.

Names of Artists

REPRESENTED IN THIS SALE.

—• • •— ---

AMERICAN.

BIERSTADT.	HART, (JAS.)
BAKER, (G.)	HASELTINE.
BOUGHTON.	HALL.
BROWN, (J. G.)	HICKS.
BABCOCK.	HOTCHKISS.
BENSON.	HENNESEY.
BARROW.	INNES.
CHURCH.	JOHNSON, (E.)
COLE.	KENSETT.
CASILEAR.	KNAPP.
COLMAN.	LEUTZE.
CROPSEY.	LAMBDIN.
CHAMPNEY.	LANG.
DURAND.	MIGNOT.
DELLAAS.	RICHARDS, (W. T.)
EDMONDS.	RUGGLES.
EHNINGER,	SUYDAM.
FALCONER.	STAIGG.
GIFFORD, (R. S.)	TAIT.
GRAY.	TILTON.
GIGNOUX.	WHITTREDGE.
HUNTINGTON.	WHITE.
HUBBARD.	WARREN.
HART, (W.)	WILLIAMSON.
	WYANT.

FOREIGN.

HODDINGTON.	HERDLING.
BOLDINI.	JACQUE.
HUHLER.	KOEK-KOEK.
BOUCHENVILLE.	KENNEDY.
HAADEN.	LAMBINET.
BURGERS.	LOUINEAU,
BACHEREAU.	LESREL.
BOUDIN.	LEYENDECKER.
CASTRES.	LE ROUX.
CASTAN.	MADRAZO.
COOMANS.	MUTRIE.
COUTOURIER.	MUNIER.
DUVERGER.	MARIS.
DILLENS.	PLASSAN.
DUNOUY.	PASCUTTI.
DELA BRELY.	REDOUET.
EGUSQUIZA.	RICHET.
FRERE, (ED.)	SCHELFOUT.
FRERE, (T.)	SINKEL.
GLAIZE.	VERHAS.
GEBBA.	WYNANTS.
HUBNER.	

First Evening's Sale.

WEDNESDAY, MARCH 24TH.

— ••• —

1. WILLIAMSON (A.) A.,   New York. *Waite*
   18   Morning Glories.

2. HART (WM.) N. A.,   New York. *Hinton*
   43   Autumn.

3. LAMBDIN (G. C.) N. A.,   Philadelphia. *Pease*
   28   Young America.

4. FALCONER (J. M.) A.,   New York. *Pease*
   2,3   Kenilworth.

5. HENNESSEY (W. J.) N. A.,   London. *Powell*
   75   Alone !

Moore 6. BROWN (J. G.) N. A., New York.
30   Childhood.   *3 0*

Swermore 7. HICKS (T.) N. A., New York.
  Zouave Encampment. *35*

J T Soutter 8. RICHARDS (W. T.) N. A., Philadelphia.
  Study from Nature. *50*

W W Webb 9. LANG (LOUIS) N. A., New York.
  The Wreath. *40*

J Snedecor 10. HART (JAS. M.) N. A., New York.
  Adirondack Lake. *75*

Pease 11. EHNINGER (J. W.) N. A., New York.
  The Blue Dress. *40*

C Volney 12. SUYDAM (J. A.) N. A., deceased, New York.
  Twilight. *32*

7

13. HALL (G. H.) N. A.,   New York
It A Hurtbut "Miles Standish."   *50*

14. TAIT (A. F.) N. A.,   New York.
J H Ballentine Partridge and Young.   *100*

15. GRAY (H. P.) Ex P. N. A.,   New York.
W A(Russell "Good-bye."   *32*

16. CASILEAR (J. W.) N. A..   New York.
Sure mere. On the Hills.   *60*

17. HUNTINGTON (D.) Ex P. N. A., New York.
T Thornell Ariadne.   *92*

18. KENSETT (J. F.) N. A., deceased, New York.
Mrs Fahnifie Newport.   *85*

19. BAKER (G. A.) N. A.,   New York.
R6 mount A Young Girl.   *150*

20. BIERSTADT (A.) N. A.,   New York.

Ibache   Colorado River.   200

21. SUYDAM (J. A.) N. A., deceased, New York.

W A Russell On the Hudson River.   52

22. BURGER (H.),   Paris.

R Graves   In the Conservatory.   130

23. HUBBARD (R. W.) N. A.,   New York.

P H Ballentine Crossing the Brook.   80

24. KNAPP (C. W.),   New York.

P H Ballentine A Sunny Morning.   45

25. GIFFORD (S. R.) N. A.,   New York.

Moore   Mt. Mansfield.   205

26. LANG (LOUIS), N. A.,   New York.

T Dickson In the Flowers.   95

27. BOUGHTON (G. H.) N. A.,   London.

E J'Southmayd Winter Morning.   330

28. STAIGG (R. M.) N. A.,   Boston.

J Williams Reading Novels.   5Q

29. SINKEL,   Dusseldorf.

A Torsey St. Cecilia.   50

30. DUVERGER,   Paris.

Mrs E Q Wolfe The Young Bird.   325

31. LAMBINET (E.),   Paris.

A Babcock Landscape.   180

31a.CASTRES (E.),   Paris.

J F Slade The Major-Domo.   135

32. HERDLING,   Frankfurt.

Huntington Winter.   125

33. LESREL (A.),   Paris.

Goale Jr. A. Halberdier, 15th Century, *190*

34. PLASSAN (E.),   Paris.

Peabody Children's Breakfast.   *170*

35. MADRAZO,   Paris.

F. Tomes Fruit Market—Grenada.   *205*

36. DILLENS (AD.),   Brussels.

Walter Mother's Kiss.   *150*

36a. GIFFORD (S. R.) N. A.,   New York.

Webb Catskill Clove.   *140*

37. HUBNER (JULIUS),   Dusseldorf.

J Tuttle Smith "Probabilities."   *78*

38. BAADER (L. M.),   Paris.

J J Stone Traveling Tinker, 15th Century. *190*

39. HASELTINE (W. S.) N. A.,   Rome.

dm Hmlow Wood Scene.   45'

40. CROPSEY (J. F.), N. A.,   New York.

7 Dichson English Landscape.   67

41. HUNTINGTON (D.) Ex P. N. A., New York.

S Tousey Brook by the Meadows. 295'

42. HASELTINE (W. S.) N. A.,   Rome.

dm Hmlow Coast of Capri.   65'

43. CASILEAR (J. W.) N. A.,   New York.

Francis Skiddy Genesee Meadows.   390

44. KENSETT (J. F.) N. A., deceased, New York.

Osborne After a Storm, Mass. Coast. 1000

45. DURAND (A. B.) Ex P. N. A., New York.

S Babcock Catskill Scenery.   750

P H Ballentine

46. BODDINGTON (H. J.) deceased,   London.

    Autumn Evening in Wales.. *9 10"*

Penfold

47. HART (WILLIAM) N. A.,   New York.

    Close of the Day, Mt. Desert. *26 5*

Allen

48. LAMBDIN (G. C.) N. A.,   Philadelphia.

    The Camelia.   *150*

Walker

46a. GESSA (S.),   Paris.

    Interior French Kitchen.   *160*

Mr Hinton

49. CHURCH (F. E.) N. A.,   New York.

    South American Scenery. *262 5*

J Balcarch

50. KOEK-KOEK (B. C.) deceased,   Holland.

    Dutch Landscape.   *5 60*

J J Souter

51. MARIS (W.),   The Hague.

    Cows in a Landscape.   *2 35*

Moore

52. INNES (GEO.) N. A.,   Rome.

The Edge of a Wood—Evening. *170*

~~Samuels~~

52a. COOMANS (J.),   Paris.

Repose—Pompeian Girl.   *340*

Babcock

53. SUYDAM (J. A.) N. A., deceased, New York.

Moonrise on the Coast.   *250*

Dr Hinton

54. HICKS (T.) N. A.,   New York.

Italian Scene.   *120*

Harper

55. BOUCHERVILLE (A. DE),   Paris.

Child with Lilacs.   *200*

Wm a Camp

56. COLMAN (S.) N. A..   New York.

Lake—White Mountains.   *180*

Clark

56a. FRERE (THEO.),   Paris.

Street in Cairo.   *175*

Pease

.3

57. KNAPP (C. W.), New York.

Landscape. *40*

R L Stuart

58. MUTRIE (Miss A. F.), London.

Flowers upon a Bank. *200*

Tho Dickson

59. ALBOY-REBOUET (A.), Paris.

Going to the Hunt. *110*

Powell

60. BEAUVERIE (C. J.), Paris.

French Landscape. *70*

Moore

61. KENSETT (J. F.) N. A., deceased, New York.

English Scene. *95*

Walker

61a. LEYENDECKER (PAUL), Paris.

Homer reciting his Odes. *130*

Van Valkenburgh

62. FRERE (E.), Paris.

The Christmas Drum. *885*

\ :4. .34

63. BIERSTADT (A.) N. A., New York.

\ View of Dusseldorf. *410*

Graves \ \
64. WYNANTS, deceased, Holland.

. View of Ghent. (Horses, &c., by Verboeckhoven.) *130*

R
65. WILLIAMSON (A.) A., New York. *40*

' ' Grapes.

Peabody
65a. EGUSQUIZA (R.), Paris. *75* '

\' For the Promenade.

Powell \
66. LOUINEAU, deceased, Rome. *35* '

Contemplation.

H W Robbins
67. TILTON (J. R.), Rome. *50*

\ Lake Orta (Italy).

Babcock
68. RICHARDS (W. T.) N. A., Philadelphia. *340*

On the Coast.

J H Ballentine [16]

68a. GIGNOUX (R.), New York.

Winter Landscape. *3/5*

T Dickson

69. BENSON (E.) A., New York.

Copy from Titian. *45*

Dickson

70. LAMBDIN (G. C.) N. A., Philadelphia.

Study of Flowers. *75*

T Thornell

71. HOTCHKISS (T.) deceased, New York.

Creek in the Highlands. *1/*

P H Ballentine

72. HUBBARD (R. W.) N. A., New York.

Lake Dunmore. *47*

T Thornell

73. JACQUE (CHAS.), Paris.

Study of Flowers. *11*

T Thornell

74. KNAPP (C. W.), New York.

Mountain Brook. *2/*

Second Evening's Sale.

THURSDAY, MARCH 25TH.

———•••———

Woodbury

75. CHAMPNEY (B.),   Boston.

    White Mt. Scene.   *5 5*

Howner

76. WARREN (A. W.) A., deceased, New York.   *6 5*

    Old Houses—Brooklyn.

77. RUGGLES (S.), deceased,   New York.

    White Mt. Scene.

Brett

78. HENNESSY (W. J.) N. A.,   London.

    Morning Prayer.   *4 2*

Livermore

79. WHITTREDGE (W.) P. N. A.,   New York.   *5 0*

    In the Catskills.

J T Swift

80. DE HAAS (M. F. DE) N. A.,   New York.

A Fresh Breeze.   *77*

Powell

81. GIGNOUX (R.) N. A.,   New York.

Old Fulton Market.   *42*

E C Cowdin

82. TAIT (A. F.) N. A.,   New York.

Young Quail.   *62*

Wait

83. MIGNOT (L. R.) N. A., deceased, New York.

Tropical Scene.   *100*

J T Swift

84. STAIGG (R. M.) N. A.,   Boston.

Little Street Sweeper.   *82*

Cowdin

85. HALL (G. H.) N. A.,   New York.

" Priscilla."   *100*

Cowdin

86. HALL (G. H.) N. A.,   New York.

"John Arden."   *100*

J E Burril

87. GIFFORD (S. R.) N. A., New York.
       Autumn—White Mt.   *83.*

Dickson

88. HICKS (T.) N. A., New York.
       Near Fontainbleau.   *60*

Moore

89. KENSETT (J. F.) N. A., deceased, New York.
       Twilight.   *103*

Burril

90. HASELTINE (W. S.) N. A., Rome.
       Hudson River.   *130*

C Delmonico

91. EGUSQUIZA (R.), Paris.
       After the Bal Masque.   *72*

Allen

92. WHITE (EDWIN) N. A., New York.
       In the Barn.   *26*

C H Welling

92a. SHELFOUT, deceased, Holland.   *72*
       View of Haarlem.

Burril

93. FRERE (T.),   Paris.

Banks of the Bosphorus. *155'*

R Seaman

94. BROWN (J. G.) N. A.,   New York.

At the Window.   *70*

Henry Smith

95. BENSON (E.) A.,   New York.

Coming Night.   *47*

J T Swift

96. COUTOURIER,   Paris.

Waiting for Supper.   *130*

S. Tousey

97. HUBNER (JULIUS),   Dusseldorf.

The Lesson.   *160*

Southmayd

98. JOHNSON (E.) N. A.,   New York.

"Give Me a Penny."   *290*

Burril

99. CASILEAR (J. W.) N. A,   New York.

Swiss Mountains.   *260*

Thornell

100. HASELTINE (W. S.) N. A.,   Rome. *152*

Coast of Maine.

Burril

101. DURAND (A. B.) Ex P. N. A., New York. *100*

Morning.

Burril

102. DURAND (A. B.) Ex P. N. A., New York. *100*

Evening.

A W C Wheeler

103. JOHNSON (E. KILLINGWORTH), London.

Striking a Light (Water Color).   *160*

Avery

104. BABCOCK (W. P.),   Boston.   *25*

Ideal Head.

C Delmonico

105. BACHEREAU (V.),   Paris.   *120*

The Letter (Empire costume).

Camp

106. BAKER (G. A.) N. A.,   New York.

Rose Leaves.   *235*

L Turnure)) 3,3 .

107. KOEK-KOEK (B. C.), deceased,   Holland.

A Dutch Farm-house.   *150*

Old Munn

108. LEYENDECKER (PAUL),   Paris.

In the Garden of Plants (Paris). *220*

R L Stuart

109. PLASSAN (E.),   Paris.

The Declaration.   *565*

Parsons

110. GIFFORD (S. R.) N. A.,   New York.

Sunset on the Lake.   *260*

Van Valfenburgh

111. CASTAN (E.),   Paris.

Prayer.   *370*

Harper

112. BOLDINI,   Paris.

Bois-de-Boulogne.   *160*

Downer

113. BOUCHERVILLE (A. De),   Paris.

In the Studio.   *230*

320

114. PASCUTTI (A.), Rome.

The Duet.

B Hazard *125'*

115. LEROUX (EUG.), Paris.

A Lady of the 1st Empire.

C Frost *130*

116. RICHET (E.), Paris.

Children in the Wood.

B Blakeman

117. KENNEDY (E. SHEEARD), London.

The Fate of the Boquet. *290*

Munn

118. GLAIZE (P. L.), Paris.

The Squirrel. *180*

I T Swift

119. JAZET (P. L.), Paris.

The Guard (Nuremberg, 16th century). *135'*

Schaus

120. LAMBINET (E.), Paris.

French Landscape. *230*

1

121. LANG (LOUIS) N. A.,   New York.

Le Pensorosa.

Southmayd

122. BOUGHTON (G. H.) N. A.,   London.

Christmas Morning (Brittany). *1625*

W Richmond

123. BUHLER (ZUBER),   Paris.

Just Up.   *700*

W E Strong

124. CROPSEY (J. F.), N. A.,   New York.

Cottage at Lulworth (England). *150*

W J Garrison

125. EDMUNDS (F. W.) N. A., dec'd, New York.

"All Talk and no Work." *220*

R Seaman

126. COLE (THOS.) N. A., deceased,   Catskill.

Evening (A composition). *280*

Babcock

127. WHITTREDGE (W.) P. N. A., New York.

View near Dobbs' Ferry. *225*

Allen

128. VERHAS (JAN.),   Brussels.

Aid and Protection.   *180*

Stewart Meyer

129. LEUTZE (E.) N. A., deceased, Dusseldorf.   *460*

The Petitioner.

Allen

130. LANG (LOUIS), N. A.,   New York.   *85*

Roman Girl.

R L Stuart

131. MIGNOT (L. R.) N. A., deceased, New York.   *500*

Village in South America (The figures by E. JOHNSON).

Babcock

132. KENSETT (J. F.) N. A., deceased, New York.   *1600*

Hudson River, from Fort Putnam.

Bigelow

133. BIERSTADT (A.) N. A.,   New York.   *2100*

Rocky Mountain Scenery.

Bigelow Babcock

134. CHURCH (F. C.) N. A.,   New York.   *900*

Evening (New England).

Penfold

135. GIGNOUX (R.) N. A., New York.
 Winter Sunset. *505*

Dickson

136. CASILEAR (J. W.) N. A., New York.
 The Wetterhorn (Swiss). *560*

Walker

137. KNAPP (C. W.), New York.
 A Hazy Morning. *60*

Wilkinson

138. BARROW (J. D.) A., New York.
 Skaneateles Lake (Evening). *45*

Peabody

139. MUNGER (E), Paris.
 Home from School. *170*

Garrison

140. SCHLESINGER, Dusseldorf.
 Return from the Fields. *170*

R L Stuart

141. KENSETT (J. F.) N.A., deceased, New York.
 Shrewsbury River. *1125*

Thornell

142. COLMAN (S.) N. A., New York.
 Twilight. *165*

Clark

143. WEBER (OTTO),   Berlin.
Brittany Family.   *153*

Burrel

144. CROPSEY (J. F.) N. A.,   New York.
English Cottage.   *220*

145. LECOMTE-DU-NOUY (J.),   Paris.
Girl of Athens.

C. Frost

146. FRERE (THEO.),   Paris.
River Scene (Cairo).   *132*

Nid aldrich

147. RICHARDS (W. T.) N. A.,   Philadelphia.
Study from Nature.   *200*

Henry Smith

148. BOUDIN (E.),   Paris. *90*
French Coast, with Figures.

B Hajard

149. DELA BRELY (A.),   Paris. *245*
Terrace at Versailles (Louis XIII.)

Hajard

150. WEBER (PAUL),   Philadelphia.
Fontainbleau.   *205*

W E Strong   28

151. WILLIAMSON (J.) A.,   New York.
     Study of Grapes.   35

Aldrich

152. KNAPP (C. W.),   New York.
     Evening.   40

Aldrich

153. STAIGG (R. M.) N. A.,   Boston.
     Reading the News.   175

Henry Smith

154. BENSON (E.) A.,   New York.
     " Coming Tears."   60

Dickson

155. LAMBDIN (G. C.) N. A.,   Philadelphia.
     Study of Flowers.   70

Strong

156. WYATT (A.) N. A.,   New York.
     Autumn.   100

Dundas Dick

157. HOTCHKISS (T.), deceased,   New York.
     In the Woods (Study).   55

www.ingramcontent.com/pod-product-compliance
Lightning Source LLC
Chambersburg PA
CBHW021610270326
41931CB00009B/1407